SQL for Data Analytics

Perform efficient and fast data analysis with the power of SQL

By

Rose Smith

Contents

Introduction

Chapter 1 Structure Of A Database

 1.1: Database

 1.2: Types

 1.3: Components

 1.4: Database Management System

Chapter 2: SQL Tools and Strategies

 2.1: SQL Management Server Studio for Microsoft

 2.2: MySQL Workbench

 2.3: DbVisualizer

Chapter 3: Exploring a Database in SQLite

 3.1: What precisely is SQLite?

 3.2: SQLite's Specialties

 3.3: Database Overview

Chapter 4 Getting Started with Queries

 4.1: Constructs and Queries Fundamental to SQL

Chapter 5: Turning Data Into Information

5.1: What is meant by "data transformation"?

5.2: How to Manipulate/Transform Data?

5.3: Improving Data Transformation

Chapter 6: Working on Multiple Tables

6.1: Using JOINS For Multiple Tables

6.2: Types of JOINS

6.3: Advantages of JOINS

Chapter 7 Functions

7.1: Functions

7.2: Brand-New Functions

7.3: Parameters

Chapter 8: Subqueries

8.1 What are subqueries?

8.2 Best Practices for Subquery

8.3: Guidelines for Subqueries

8.4: Various Types of Subqueries

8.5: Correlated subqueries

8.6: Comparison operators in subqueries

Chapter 9: Views

9.1: Creating a SQL VIEW

9.2: Advantages of View

9.3: Disadvantages of View

Chapter 10: Data Manipulation Language

10.1: Purpose Of Data Manipulations

10.2: Variations

Conclusion

Introduction

The Structured Query Language for Data Analysis, or SQL for Data Analysis, is an amazingly effective programming language that enables data analysts to interact with data housed in relational databases. Several businesses have developed specialized tools to swiftly get information from databases using SQL.

SQL seems to have become even more necessary for sophisticated analysts or data scientists due to the growth of data, processing capacity, and cloud data warehouses. This book exposes fresh and secret techniques for enhancing your SQL abilities, solving difficulties, and maximizing SQL as part of the workflow. SQL is widely used not only because it is a simple language but also because it can do surprisingly complicated data analysis. Its speed in creating databases and interacting with them continues to be the primary reason for its widespread use. The improvement of a company's products and services via the use of data analysis makes the company's customers feel more satisfied. The Data Analysis procedure entails gathering and organizing large amounts of data to derive valuable knowledge since this assists in making crucial choices necessary to succeed in business. Technology development has enabled the discovery of important factors and predicting patterns and trends, all of which contribute to increased corporate efficiency. It makes it simpler/easier to make informed decisions. This method has made it possible for the sector to direct its development by evaluating significant information to make important business choices. When companies try to anticipate their future business needs by mining the previous information stored in their databases, data analysis has become an increasingly important tool for spotting patterns and trends.

Hence this book will allow you to use SQL as a bridge between end users and a more complicated data storage system which would be more approachable to specialists and data scientists since it can communicate directly with databases created in these languages.

Chapter 1 Structure Of A Database

In plain language, data can be considered facts about any subject under consideration. Some examples of records relevant to you include your name, maturity level, height, weight, and other similar details. A photo, image, file, or PDF can also represent data, among other things.

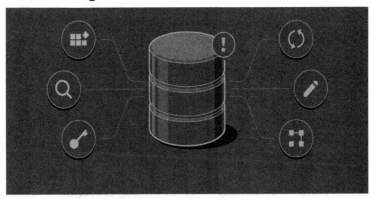

1.1: Database

A database is a prepared compilation of various types of data. They allow for storage and data manipulation in an electronic format. Databases make data management easy. Let us talk about a database example: A database is utilized by an online phone directory to store information regarding individuals, including their phone numbers and other contact information. Your power provider likely uses a database to handle billing, customer-related issues, fault data, and other administrative tasks. Let us also consider Facebook. It must save, manipulate, and display data relating to members, their mates, member events, messages, ad campaigns, and much more. Regarding the applications of databases, we can present an infinite number of examples.

In SQL Server, a cluster of tables is what constitutes a database. Each table holds its own unique set of data in an organized format. A group of rows, also known as records or tuples, and columns, also referred to as the attributes, are contained within a table. Dates, names, cash flows, and other numerical values are examples of the different kinds of information that can be included in the various columns of the table. SQL Server can be installed on a computer simultaneously in single or several instances. There is no maximum value to the number of databases a single instance of SQL Server can host. One or more groups of object ownership can be found within a database and are referred to as schemas. Tables, views, or stored procedures are examples of database items that can be found contained within each schema. Some items are stored within the database and not stored within a schema. Examples of these objects include certificates and asymmetric keys. Please refer to Tables for further details regarding the creation of tables. The file system is where SQL Server databases get stored in their file form. Files can be organized into file groups. Database Files & Filegroups is where you may find additional information about databases' files and filegroups.

An individual is referred to as a login once they successfully log in to a SQL statement. A person is a database user if granted access to the associated database. A login may serve as the foundation for a database user. A database user not based on login can be formed if enclosed databases are enabled.

This user does not require a login. Please go to the CREATE USER page for further information regarding users (Transact-SQL). It is likely to grant a user consent to view the objects stored in a database if that user already has access to it. Even though rights can be granted to individual users, we advocate creating database responsibilities, adding database customers to the positions, and then granting appropriate access to the roles. Individual users can also be granted permission. Maintaining consistent and intelligible permissions is far simpler if they are granted to roles rather than individual users, particularly when the number of users continues to expand and fluctuate.

1.2: Types

The following are some common varieties of databases:

Distributed databases

A dispersed database is a database that receives contributions from a common database and information acquired by local computers. Distributed databases are also known as networked databases. The data for this kind of database system is not kept in a single location but dispersed among several different businesses. Relational databases are characterized by the practice of defining database relationships using table-based structures. It is also known as Relational DBMS, the type of database management system that is the most widely used industry. MySQL, Oracle, and the Microsoft SQL Server database are all examples of databases that an RDBMS system can manage. Object-oriented databases are a form of database that may be used on computers and support storing all types of data. The information is kept in the form of items during storage. The characteristics and methods of the objects stored in the database will define what should be done with the data. One example of an object-oriented relational database management system is PostgreSQL. Centrally located Database Users can come from various backgrounds because it is in a central area. The application processes that allow users to access the material even when in a remote place are stored in computer databases of this kind.

Open-source databases

These are the types of databases that contain information pertinent to business operations. The fields of marketing, labor relations, customer support, and database management are the most common applications for its utilization.

Databases stored in the cloud

A database stored in the cloud is a database that is customized or built specifically for a virtualized environment. Many benefits are associated with using a database hosted in the cloud, and some of these benefits might pay for data storage and bandwidth. In addition to this, it provides scalability on demand as well as high availability.

Data warehouses

The purpose of a warehouse is to assist in creating one version of the truth that an organization can use for strategic planning and forecasting. A data warehouse is a type of information system that stores data that has been accumulated over time and may be accessed from a single source or several sources. The reporting and analyzing procedures of the firm might be made more straightforward by utilizing the Data Warehouse concept.

NoSQL databases

A NoSQL database is a sort of database that is used for managing big, dispersed data collections. Relational databases can efficiently solve several performance issues associated with big data. The assessment of vast sums of unstructured data can be performed extremely quickly using this computer database.

Graph databases

A graph-oriented database is a database that stores, maps, and queries relationships by making use of graph theory. Computer databases of this nature are typically used to investigate interconnections. For instance, a company may utilize a knowledge graph to harvest information about customers from media platforms using those customers' accounts.

OLTP Database

OLTP databases are another database that can perform quick query processing and keep data integrity for multi-access scenarios. OLTP databases are also known as online transaction processing databases.

Private Database

A private database is a type of database that can be used to store data on personal computers. Personal databases are often smaller and easier to operate than corporate databases. A relatively small number of people have access to the data, most of which is utilized by the same function of the company.

Multimodal database

A multimodal database is a computational platform that provides different data models that specify how specific knowledge and information included within a database should be organized and arranged. This type of database is also known as a multimodal database.

Document/JSON database

The data in a pdf file database are stored in document collections, and the formats XML, JSON, and BSON are typically used to store and retrieve the data. One entry can store unlimited data in the user's data type (or data type). The "parent-child" connection organizes and stores the data in a hierarchical database management system (DBMS). Its structure is like a tree, with nodes standing in for records and branches for the various fields. One example of a hierarchical database is Windows XP's registry, which is used by that operating system.

Network DBMS

This kind of database management system can support many-to-many relations. Typically, this ends in producing complicated database structures. An example of a system for managing databases that follow the network model is called RDM Server.

1.3: Components

A database is comprised of the following five primary parts: The term "hardware" refers to a collection of tangible electronic devices, such as computers, input/output devices, storage devices, and so on. This links computers and the systems that exist in the real world.

Software

It refers to a collection of programs that are utilized in the process of managing and controlling the database. It covers the DBMS, the software platform, and the computer system used to share the information among users and the application applications required to access data stored in the database. Also included in this category is the software used to communicate useful information. Data are facts that have not been sorted or organized in any way, and before they can have any significance, they need to be processed. Data can be straightforward while chaotic unless the proper organization is applied. Facts, observations, views, numbers, letters, symbols, images, and so on are data types.

The word "procedure" refers to a set of rules and instructions that can be followed to effectively use the database management system (DBMS). It is the process of developing and executing the database with the help of documented techniques, which gives you the ability to direct the users who plan and maintain it.

Database Access Language

Database Access extracts content to and from the databases, enters new data, alters current data, or gets required data from DBMS. Database Access language can also be used to retrieve data needed from DBMS. The user composes a set of commands using a database server language and then sends these instructions to the database.

A database that has been structured correctly:

1. Lessens the quantity of space required on the disc by removing redundant data.

2. Ensures the correctness and reliability of the data.
3. Offers access to the information in helpful ways.
4. To create an effective and helpful database, it is necessary to follow the appropriate method.
5. Analysis of the requirements, often known as determining the function of your database
6. Clustering data into tables
7. Identifying the essential keys and analyzing their relationships
8. Normalization for table standardization

1.4: Database Management System

The acronym "DBMS" stands for "database management system," which refers to a collection of computer applications that enables people to access databases, alter data, generate reports, and depict data. In addition, it helps control who can access the database. The idea of database management systems is not new; in fact, the first systems of this kind were implemented in the 1960s. It is believed that Charles Bachman's Integrated File System (IDS) was the very first database management system in the history of the world. With time, database technologies underwent significant evolutions, while databases' utilization and expected capabilities experienced enormous increases.

The following are some of the most significant landmarks from throughout history:

In 1960, Charles Bachman created the first database management system.

1970, Codd introduced the Information Management System from IBM (IMS).

Peter Chen conceived of and provided the initial definition for what is now commonly referred to as the entity-relationship model (ER model) in 1976.

In 1980, the relational model was recognized as a necessary component of databases everywhere. 1985 was the year that object-oriented database management systems were developed. 1990, The first implementation of object-oriented programming in relational database management systems. In 1991, Microsoft released MS Contact, a personal database management system, quickly becoming the dominant personal DBMS product on the market. In 1995, The very first database applications to run on the Internet. 1997, XML was applied for database processing. A growing number of manufacturers are beginning to include XML in their DBMS systems.

DBMS has many benefits, one of which is storing and retrieving data using many methods. A database management system (DBMS) acts as an effective manager that can balance the requirements of numerous applications that use the same data. Procedures for the administration of standardized data. Programmers working on applications are never shown the specifics of how data is represented or stored. A database management system makes use of a variety of robust features to store or retrieve data effectively. Provides both the Integrity and Security of Data. The database management system (DBMS) implements integrity constraints to achieve a high level of prevention against unauthorized data access. A database management system (DBMS) is responsible for scheduling access control toward the data so that only one user can view the same data simultaneously. Time Saved During the Application Development Process.

Chapter 2: SQL Tools and Strategies

If you're a database developer or perhaps an administrator, you are likely interested in finding out which SQL editor tool provides the most effective assistance in managing your database. You are looking for a solution that offers competitive pricing, superior customer assistance, and the appropriate deployment choices. However, there are a lot of different SQL editing tools available, and not every one of them could be suitable for your specific requirements. SQL was established in the 1970s, but it has gone a long way since its days as the exclusive purview of code experts, thanks to the proliferation of various IT management solutions. It began as a tool developed to edit data in IBM's System R, but it has since evolved into one of the computer languages used most often worldwide. 56.6 percent of all developers around the globe utilize SQL.

In the end, such a universal database query language is simple to pick up and may be used with most engines. Because of its lightning-fast speed, it is also quite advantageous when manipulating data in various ways. In addition, SQL engines power many of today's most prominent business intelligence solutions across various sectors. Because AI has the intrinsic potential to extract useful patterns and insights from any amount of data, businesses are scrambling to take full advantage of all these capabilities to accelerate their development.

However, having knowledge of SQL by itself is not sufficient. You will require SQL editing tools to use for the data manipulation efforts so that you may exploit it. These act as hubs via which you can submit instructions that will assist you in communicating with the database system with which you are working. After reading this book, you will better understand the existing SQL editing solutions available on the market. It ought to make it possible for you to figure out which ones are consistent with the databases and which ones will give you the tools you need to effectively query & manage your data.

2.1: SQL Management Server Studio for Microsoft

A database administration tool for SQL servers, Azure SQL Data Warehouse, Azure SQL Database, and Parallel Data Warehouse is called Microsoft SQL Management Server Studio (SSMS). The properly connected script editor and powerful query statistics reporting features on this platform make it ideal for developers who spend a significant amount of time with database administration & sophisticated settings.

It contains a complete set of tools, including query editing through IntelliSense, table designer, object explorers, script production, and object scripting. The platform provides real-time reporting on clients' and lives query statistics so you can obtain a full picture of the overall health of your database. Security is made simple with Microsoft SSMS, which is another cool feature. It includes a vulnerability analysis and unique security features. You will have total control over encryptions in this manner. Microsoft SSMS, like every product, has a drawback: the platform doesn't support Linux & macOS. To utilize it, you must ensure that your devices are Windows OS-compatible.

Key Features of the Integrated Script Editor in Microsoft SQL Management Server Studio.

- The code editor included in Microsoft SSMS supports Transact-SQL, DMX, MDX, and XML/A. Additionally, it offers users various pre-made themes and bespoke templates that speed up programming more than before. And to top everything off, SSMS has an embedded source control system so you can keep copies of your scripts updated.

- Object Navigator Users of this platform may examine and manage items on all sorts of servers using the object explorer. Thanks to its hierarchical user interface, each instance on your server may be easily controlled. For quicker searches, you may also filter things based on certain criteria.
- New Activity Monitor. It's practically hard to manually keep track of everything that occurs in your database. The platform's new activity tracker will record every action you take in real-time for simpler monitoring, making it easier for you to distinguish changes in the server, whether they include data retrieval, removal, or modifications.

2.2: MySQL Workbench

A visual editor called MySQL Workbench combines database management, SQL programming, and data modeling into one user interface. You may use any OS to design, construct, and manage databases graphically. The software may also help you with database backup, reverse engineering, and server setup. The portability of this solution will provide distributed database architects & developers the advantage they need to streamline operations while safeguarding data. MySQL Workbench's database migration features facilitate data movement to and from Microsoft SQL Server, Sybase ASE, Microsoft Access, PostgreSQL, and other RDBMS tables. Because this software enables developers to see their databases, implement change management strategies, and create database documentation, the danger of human mistakes is also decreased. Finally, MySQL Workbench has a SQL snippet panel, the table data search panel, and results within windows to reduce the need to switch programs.

MySQL Workbench Visual SQL Editor's main features.

- Developers may create, amend, and execute queries using the visual SQL editor in MySQL

Workbench. It is fantastic since it lets you preview the modifications before implementing them. Moreover, color syntax highlighting, context-sensitive support, and auto-complete capabilities make debugging and writing SQL queries significantly quicker.

- Database Management. In addition to giving you tools for authoring SQL, MySQL Workbench also includes a suite for managing databases. You can now set up servers, check logs, and easily audit your databases. It also has a system status function that lets you quickly see your MySQL environment's health indicators, such as security and memory utilization.

- Performance Evaluation. The dashboard MySQL Workbench provides allows users to see the status of the queries, network latency, client timing, and index utilization. It makes it easier to identify potential strategies for improving SQL performance.

2.3: DbVisualizer

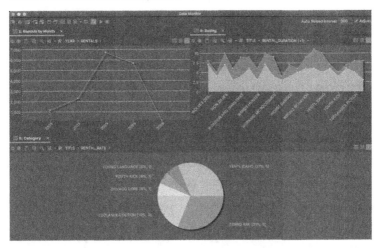

DbVisualizer, a user-friendly multi-database program. It offers customers options to manage databases throughout many platforms via a single portal, much like other leading platforms. DbVisualizer is among the most well-liked since it is compatible with all major OSes. Additionally, it offers several connectors with other products, making it a preferred platform for many developers, analysts, database administrators, and programmers in businesses of all sizes and sectors.

Among the key features are modules for query generation, SQL editing, database server administration, database connection management, and database object management. Task monitoring, charts, reference graphs, SQL history, SSH, & command line interface are standard features. You may combine the program with other tools in the digital architecture thanks to its on-premises deployment and Open API capabilities. It smoothly integrates with various systems, including Amazon Redshift, Oracle, Yellowbrick, MySQL, Derby, and MimerSQL. The platform provides a free edition with a few but extremely functional capabilities, including connection management and an interface that can be customized. Paid packages begin at $197. The pro versions are available for a free trial.

Key features of the Dynamic SQL Tools in DbVisualizer.

- The platform has constructed modules for SQL queries & makes it simple to update and run SQL statements. You may even create such with the help of these simple tools without any prior technical expertise in SQL syntax. You can interact with some visual user interface tools using simple drag & drop controls.

- Simple coding. The SQL editing tool in DbVisualizer contains a built-in error highlighting function. Users can easily identify and address problems as a result. Additionally, its autocomplete function anticipates some codes and provides several choices. Thus, this expedites the whole procedure.
- Strong monitoring and security features. DbVisualizer uses among the most rigorous security precautions for its system is one of its main advantages. They use SSH to secure your data and automatically preserve your work so that you may continue where users left off. Additionally, developers may easily follow and monitor other jobs and the system's condition even when working on another activity, owing to its monitoring tools. It serves as a

focal point for all database-related operations.

Chapter 3: Exploring a Database in SQLite

The SQLite database engine is a self-contained, platform-independent, zero-configuration, transactional database engine implemented by the SQLite software library. However, this expansion is in terms of recognition and has nothing to do with the size of SQLite; it is one of the database engines that is expanding at one of the quickest rates. The SQLite source code is available for anybody to see and modify.

3.1: What precisely is SQLite?

SQLite is a library that provides a self-contained, zero-configuration, transaction SQL database engine. SQLite is also known as a transaction SQL database engine. It is a database that does not need to be set up on your system as other databases do since it is zero-configured, which implies that it comes out of the box.

In SQLite, you may connect it statically or dynamically with your application, depending on the needs of your business. SQLite has immediate access to the files that make up its storage.

Why use SQLite?

Operating SQLite databases do not require a separate server program or computer system.

- SQLite is distributed with zero configuration, which indicates that it does not need any initialization or management.
- A full SQLite database may be kept in a single disc file compatible with several operating systems.
- SQLite is a highly compact and lightweight database management system, weighing in at less than 400 kilobytes when fully configured and less than 250 kilobytes when extra features are disabled.

- SQLite does not need any external dependencies since it is a self-contained program.
- Transactions in SQLite completely comply with the ACID standard, which enables safe access from many processes or threads.
- Most of the SQL query capabilities that are included in the SQL92 (SQL2) standard are supported by SQLite.
- SQLite is designed in ANSI-C and offers an API that is straightforward to work with.
- SQLite is accessible on Windows, in addition to UNIX (Linux, Mac OS (Operating System) X, Android, and iOS) (Win32, WinCE, WinRT).

3.2: SQLite's Specialties

It describes SQLite's uncommon features that set it apart from other SQL database engines.

Zero-Configuration

SQLite is not "installed" before usage. No "setup" exists. There is no server to run, stop, or configure. Administrators do not need to build new database instances or provide user rights. SQLite is configuration-less. Nothing is needed to indicate the system SQLite is functioning. A system breakdown or power loss requires no intervention. No problems exist.

Other database engines work well once started. Installation and setup might be daunting.

Serverless

Most SQL database systems are server-based. Programs that access the database use interposed communication (usually TCP/IP) to submit queries and get responses. SQLite works differently. SQLite reads and writes straight from database files on the disc. No server process exists.

Serverless has pros and cons. There is no separate server procedure to install, configure, activate, administer, or debug. SQLite is "zero-configuration" because of this. SQLite program does not need administrative help to set up the database engine. Any disk-accessible software may utilize SQLite.

A server-based database engine can defend against client application issues since stray pointers cannot affect server memory. A server may manage database access more precisely as a single permanent process, enabling finer grain lock and improved concurrency.

Client/server SQL databases are common. SQLite seems to be the only serverless database that enables many apps to access it simultaneously.

DB File

An SQLite database is a single disc file that can be placed anywhere. SQLite can access the disc file and the database. SQLite may alter the database if the disc file and directory are readable. Sharing database files is easy through USB (Universal Serial Bus) or email.

Other SQL databases hold data in several files. Often, only the DBS can access these files. It is more secure but tougher to reach. SQL database engines may circumvent the filesystem and write straight to the disc. It increases performance but complicates setup and maintenance.

Cross-platform stable database

Cross-platform SQLite files. A database file produced on one system may be utilized on a different architecture. 32-bit or 64-bit, big-endian or little-endian is irrelevant. Same file format on all devices. The latest models of SQLite may read and modify older database files because the developers have promised to make the file types stable and backward compatible.

Most SQL database engines need you to dump and reload the database when switching platforms or updating software.

Compact

The SQLite library is less than 500KiB when optimized. Unneeded functionality may be deactivated at compile time to decrease library size to around 300KiB.

Most SQL databases are bigger. IBM's newly launched Cloudscape DBS is a 2MiB jar file, an enormous amount bigger than SQLite. Firebird's client library is 350KiB. That is as large as SQLite without the database engine. Oracle's 450KiB Berkeley DB library lacks SQL capability, giving just key/value pairs.

Typing manifest

SQL databases employ static typing. Each table column has a datatype, and only that datatype's values are permitted. SQLite's manifest type relaxes this constraint. In manifest coding, the datatype belongs to the value, not the column. SQLite supports storing any datatype in any column, independent of its defined type. Exceptions: INTEGER PRIMARY KEY columns hold only integers. When possible, SQLite coerces values into the column's stated datatype.

We believe SQL permits manifest typing. Most SQL database systems are statically typed; some consider SQLite's manifest typing a defect. SQLite's creators consider this a benefit. SQLite's explicit typing is an intentional design choice that has made it more dependable and simpler, particularly with dynamically typed languages like Tcl and Python.

Readable code

SQLite's source code is meant for the typical coder. All procedures, data structures, and automatic variables are well-commented. The commentary is not repeated.

Compiling SQL into virtual assembly language

Every SQLite engine assembles each SQL query into an internal data structure for execution. Most SQL engines have a complex web of interconnected structures and objects. SQLite compiles statements into a machine-language-like program. Database users can view virtual machine language by adding EXPLAIN to a query.

Virtual machines have helped SQLite's development. The virtual machine creates a clear, well-defined intersection between the front and back end of SQLite. The virtual machine helps developers debug by displaying what SQLite is attempting to accomplish with each declaration it compiles. SQLite can print each virtualized instruction and its outcome as it executes, depending on how it is compiled.

Public Domain

SQLite is open source. None of the main source codes is copyrighted. (Documentation and test code are regulated by open-source licensing.) All SQLite contributors have signed affidavits refusing copyright. It implies anybody may legally modify SQLite's source code.

Other SQLite engines have permissive licenses that enable code reuse. Other engines still are copyright-protected. Copyright legislation does not apply to SQLite.

Other SQL database engines' source code files usually include a note indicating your legal rights to read and copy them. SQLite source code has no license since it is not copyright protected.

SQLite enhances SQL in ways other database engines do not. Already mentioned: EXPLAIN and manifest types. SQLite's REPLACE and ON CONFLICT clauses offer control over constraint resolving conflict. SQLite's ATTACH and DETACH functions let you query numerous independent databases. SQLite offers APIs for adding SQL functions and collation sequences.

3.3: Database Overview

```
int sqlite3_open(
    const char *filename,     /* Database filename (UTF-8) */
    sqlite3 **ppDb            /* OUT: SQLite db handle */
);
int sqlite3_open16(
    const void *filename,     /* Database filename (UTF-16) */
    sqlite3 **ppDb            /* OUT: SQLite db handle */
);
int sqlite3_open_v2(
    const char *filename,     /* Database filename (UTF-8) */
    sqlite3 **ppDb,           /* OUT: SQLite db handle */
    int flags,                /* Flags */
    const char *zVfs          /* Name of VFS module to use */
);
```

These procedures start up an SQLite database file based on the filename parameter. For the sqlite3 open () and sqlite3 open v2() functions, the filename parameter is interpreted as UTF-8, and for the sqlite3 open16 function, it is treated as Equipment in the native byte sequence (). Even if there is a problem, the *ppDb variables typically include a database connection handle. The only exception to this rule is that a NULL rather than a reference to a sqlite3 object will be put into *ppDb if SQL fails to allocate enough memory to contain the sqlite3 object. The SQLite OK return value is determined by whether the database was opened (or created) successfully. If this is not the case, an error code will be provided. After a failure of either of the sqlite3 open () methods, you may acquire an error message in English by using either the sqlite3 errmsg() or sqlite3 errmsg16() routine. Both functions provide a 16-character error message.

The encoding that will be used by default for databases that are created using sqlite3 open () or sqlite3 open v2 is going to be UTF-8 (). If you use the sqlite3 open16() function to create a database, that database's default encoding will be UTF-16 within native byte ordering. When the data type handle is no longer necessary, the associated resources should be freed up by sending it to the sqlite3 close () function. It should be done, although a problem arose during the opening process.

The sqlite3 open v2() interface operates in the same manner as the sqlite3 open () interface, with the exception that it takes two extra arguments for more control over the newly connected database. The sqlite3 open v2() function requires that the flags argument have, at the very least, any of the three following flag combinations:

SQLITE OPEN READ-ONLY

Read-only access has been granted to the database for the time being. An error will be issued if the database in question does not already exist.

SQLITE OPEN READ-WRITE

The databases are opened for read-only and write-only access if such functionality is available or for viewing if the system software has placed write protection on the file. In either scenario, the database in question must have previously been created; otherwise, an error will be sent back.

SQLITE OPEN READ-WRITE

SQL OPEN CREATE is a combination of the two.

The collection is opened for writing and reading, and if it does not already exist, it is created during this process. The behavior is consistently applied when calling sqlite3 open () and sqlite3 open16().

In addition to the necessary flags, the optional flags that are listed below are also supported:

SQLITE OPEN URI

If this flag is turned on, the file's name may be read as a URI.

SQLITE OPEN MEMORY

The database will first be accessed in the memory rather than saved to a disc. If the shared cache mode is set, the "filename" option will be used to name the database for cache-sharing; however, if back out mode is not enabled, the "filename" argument will be ignored.

SQLITE OPEN NO MUTEX

The newly created database connection will use the "number of co" threading mode. It translates to the fact that it is OK for many threads to make use of SQLite at the same time so long as each thread makes use of a distinct database connection.

SQLITE OPEN FULLMUTEX

The newly created database connection will use the "serialized" threading mode.

SQLITE OPEN SHARED CACHE

The shared cache setting is enabled when the database is launched, which overrides the standard shared cache option supplied by sqlite3 enable shared cache ().

SQLITE OPEN PRIVATE CACHE

The shared cache is deactivated when the database is launched, which overrides the standard shared cache option supplied by the sqlite3 enable shared cache procedure ().

SQLITE OPEN EXRESCODE

"Expanded result code mode" is the state the database connection is in when it is established. To put it another way, the behavior of the database is the same as it would be if the sqlite3 extended result codes(db,1) function were run here on the database connection as immediately as the connection was formed. This flag not only forces sqlite3 open v2() to specify the mode for extended result codes but also causes that function to return an expanded result code.

SQLITE OPEN NOFOLLOW

It is forbidden for the filename of the database to include a symbolic link.

If the third argument of sqlite3 open v2() is not among the needed combinations indicated above, optionally coupled with additional SQLITE OPEN_* bits, then the behavior is undefined. The behavior is undefined if the third parameter is not one of the necessary combinations. It is possible that this behavior will not be continued into future iterations of SQLite; hence, applications should not depend on it. Older editions of SQLite have quietly disregarded excess bits in the flags input to sqlite3 open v2(). Please note that the SQLite OPEN EXCLUSIVE setting does not have any effect if used with sqlite3 open v2 (). If the database previously exists, the presence of SQLITE OPEN

EXCLUSIVE will not result in the open operation failing. The SQLite OPEN EXCLUSIVE option is designed to be used only by the VFS interface; sqlite3 open v2 is not permitted to use it ().

The name of the sqlite3 vfs object, which describes the file system protocol that the newly created database relationship should utilize, is sent as the fourth argument to the sqlite3 open v2() function. If the fourth input is the NULL pointer, the system will use the default sqlite3 of the object.

If the filename contains the string ":memory," the connection will be given its transient, in-memory database. As soon as the connection to the database is severed, this in-memory database will be deleted. It is advised that if the name of a database file begins with a ":" character, you should precede the username with a source file such as. "/" to prevent confusion.

A personal, transient on-disk database will be created if the name is a blank string. This database will be accessible only by the user. Whenever the connection to the network is severed, this personal database will be removed from existence shortly after that.

Chapter 4 Getting Started with Queries

You have probably heard of SQL, which stands for Structured Query Language if you are considering a career in business or any other sector that requires working with data. SQL was developed for the first time in the 1970s and has been the accepted practice for interacting with databases. Considering this language's potential, many of you have probably already decided to study it. Or perhaps you think it's worth your time to study it. SQL is, without a doubt, one of the most valuable talents that job seekers may possess. SQL is essential for jobs such as data analyst and data engineer because it is used daily. In some circumstances, it might not appear to be, as necessary. I am of the firm belief that understanding SQL will offer you an advantage when working with data, which will, in turn, make the decisions you make for your company more dependable. It will enable you to comfortably analyze enormous amounts of information and concisely present the results to whichever audience you choose.

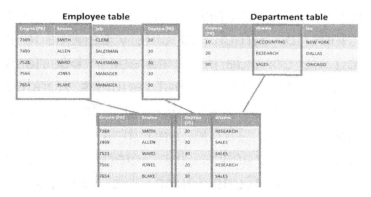

4.1: Constructs and Queries Fundamental to SQL

The following SQL clauses & functions form the basis of most SQL queries. However, there are a lot more SQL conditions and functions than can be covered in this section. In addition, the examples that have been provided here were constructed using a small dataset. In practice, you will be working with billions of rows across many different tables. There is no want to be concerned; the constructions will continue to operate similarly despite the sum of data. These fundamental queries can be used on any table in the database. Scalability is one of the primary differentiators of SQL; it distinguishes SQL from Excel and other tools that perform similarly.

The following are the fundamental components of a SQL statement:

1. Select

It would help if you employed the keyword SELECT to obtain data from a database. You can view only the data corresponding to the columns whose names you have specified (for example, customer name and age) or all the information included in the table. The FROM keyword designates the table (or tables) from which data will be obtained. Take over, for example, the scenario in which you wish to compile a list of all the clients in your database, complete with their names and email addresses.

2. Were

Imagine that you manage an online store and currently have a promotion available for clients in the United States. In this scenario, you would like to send the email to only consumers in the United States;

the list you'd like to select should contain only customers in the United States.

The WHERE clause filters select rows based on the values of one or more columns. This example is the Great nation column, which is why it isn't displayed in the results. Let's play for the second that you are solely interested in listing American women. If you use an Also keyword in the WHERE clause of your query, you can filter for many conditions at once.

3. Cases

In most cases, the Orders table of a company will include thousands of rows of information. It's possible that you won't always want to look at the total of each order. Though, you could find it more useful to classify them according to value or another criterion. You could use the CASE construct to group orders into "High" or "Low" values depending on whether the agreed price is over or below $150. It can be done by comparing the value of the order to the threshold. The CASE function is used to determine the value of each row in this query. A category is allocated to a row depending on the first circumstance (i.e., WHEN. THEN.) that evaluates to true in the conditional statement. Because the total amount of the requests with the IDs 13, 11, and 22 is greater than $150, we have designated them as 'HIGH.' The status 'LOW' has been given to the order that has ID 23. If none of the requirements are satisfied for any row, the value specified by ELSE will be used as the default return value.

```
SELECT Order_Id, Total_Value
        CASE WHEN Total_value > 150 THEN 'HIGH'
            WHEN Total_value < 150, THEN 'LOW.'
            ELSE 'MEDIUM' END as Order_Category
    FROM Orders;
```

4. Group By

When we wish to gain insights from enormous data sets, we should probably group items that are comparable together as much as possible. By grouping the data, we can use this knowledge to make educated decisions and more easily uncover trends, behaviors, or measurements. The term for this kind of grouping is aggregation, and you can accomplish this by employing the SQL GROUP BY statement. When calculating the group metric, you will typically use a function. SUM(), COUNT(), AVG(), MAX(), and MIN() are examples of aggregate functions that are often utilized (). Using these, you can do various tasks, such as determining the total costs incurred by a department or the number of workers working at each site. Let's say you decide to launch a promotion in your company in which you provide a gift voucher to the consumer who makes the highest purchase on your website. Using the SQL GROUP BY clause, you can find the client who placed the order with the highest total amount. It is quite clear that Customer Id 1213 is your most valuable client. To make the query work, all the distinct Customer Id values are selected, and then the GROUP BY operator is used to determine the aggregate cumulative total. The results are displayed with the ORDER BY 2 DESC clause in descending order based on the SUM(Total Value) column.

```
SELECT Customer_Id, SUM(Total_Value)
FROM Orders
GROUP BY Customer_Id
ORDER BY 2 DESC;
```

5. Joins

On the other hand, the Orders table does not keep any other user data, such as the customer's name or contact information. To extract the necessary data, you must create one query to the User table; otherwise, you could employ the JOIN operator. You can select data from several tables with just one query by utilizing the SQL JOIN function. In most cases, you'll join two tables by basing the connection on one or even more column values shared by both tables. In this scenario, we can make Customer Id the common field. The tables for Customers and Orders will be combined as a result. The query will now additionally return the details of the customer that you require. It does this by checking the Customer Id fields in both tables, retrieving just those rows from the second table where it detects a match for the values in the first table. It is critical to note that the user IDs

1211, 1214, and 1215 are not included in the results because the Orders table does not include any rows that match these values. You can use an OUTER JOIN if you wish to display all the values, including those that do not have a comparable match within the other table's columns. Joins are one of the essential aspects of SQL, even though grasping their logic can be challenging at times.

```
SELECT b.Customer_Name, b.Email, a.Customer_Id, SUM(Total_Value)
FROM Orders a
JOIN Customers b
ON a.Customer_id = b.Customer_Id
GROUP BY b.Customer_Name, b.Email, a.Customer_Id
ORDER BY 4 DESC;
```

6. Conditional Outcomes

If you've had a range of items, so you want to choose one of them depending on specific requirements, you may do that with a logical AND. The criterion for selecting that value must be satisfied with a "yes" answer to accomplish this. This list of conditions will be evaluated by the CASE statement for each of the possible values. If the condition is met, that value will be returned. For instance, if there is a column labeled "Grade" and you wish to select a text worth depends on the grade value, as seen in the following example:

- "Excellent" if the total score is more than 85.

- "Very Good" if the total score falls within 70 and 85 points.

- The grade is considered "Good" if it falls between 60 and 70 points.

You can accomplish this by making use of the CASE phrase. You might use this to construct some functionality in the SELECT clause, allowing you to select certain results based on certain conditions, for instance, using an if statement as an example. The CASE function can be defined in a variety of ways, including the following syntaxes:

```
CASE
    WHEN condition1 THEN result1
    WHEN condition2 THEN result2
    WHEN condition3 THEN result3

    ...

    ELSE resultn
END
```

Since SQLite is attempting to tackle a distinct problem, it cannot be directly compared to client/server SQL database engines such as MySQL, Oracle,

PostgreSQL, or SQL Server. Client/server SQL database engines work toward the goal of implementing a centralized data repository for businesses. Speed, concurrency, centralized, and control are some key concepts emphasized by them. SQLite's primary objective is to supply individual devices and programs with a local data storage option. SQLite stron misspelled gly emphasizes being economical, efficient, dependable, independent, and straightforward.

SQLite is not intended to compete with databases that use a client-server model. There is competition between SQLite and open (). People who are familiar with SQL can use the sqlite3 shellcode (or one of the many other SQLite access applications available from third parties) to perform analysis on huge datasets. Importing raw data from CSV files enables users to manipulate that data in a variety of ways, which can then be used to generate a wide variety of summary reports. Simple scripts written in Tcl or Python, both of which come pre-installed with SQLite, or simple scripts written in R or other countries using freely accessible adaptors can be used to do more advanced analyses. Analysis of website logs, analysis of sports statistics, a compilation of programming measures, and analysis of test findings are all possible applications. A significant number of bioinformatics researchers use this application of SQLite. One may accomplish the same goal by using a client-server database designed for business use. The installation and utilization of SQLite are both simplified, and the database produced is an executable track that can be saved to a USB stick or sent to a coworker. These are both advantages of using SQLite.

Chapter 5: Turning Data Into Information

For optimal outcomes, information analysis must be performed on organized and easily available data. Translating raw data into a more usable structure and format gives businesses an invaluable competitive advantage. Understand how your company can effectively convert its data to analytics.

5.1: What is meant by "data transformation"?

The process of modifying the layout, composition, or values of one's data set is referred to as data transformation. Data may transform any pipeline's first two phases in the context of data analytics initiatives. Data transformation is often performed as part of an ETL (extract, load, transform) process, which is used by businesses that keep their data warehouses on the premises of their operations. Most businesses utilize cloud-based warehouses these days because of their ability to scale computing & storage resources with a latency that can be measured in minutes or seconds. Because of the scalability of cloud platforms, businesses may bypass preload transformations, load raw data into a data warehouse, and then convert the data when it is being queried. This technique is known as ELT (transform, extract, load).

Data transformation may involve various processes, including data integration, data transfer, data warehousing, & data wrangling. A data transformation can be constructive (such as copying, adding, and replicating data), destructive (such as removing fields & records), aesthetic (such as standardizing salutations as well as street names), or structural (moving, renaming, and combining columns in a database). An organization has several options available to it in terms of ETL tools that may streamline the process of transforming data. Data transformation is a common task for data engineers, data analysts, & data scientists. These professionals often use scripting languages like Python and otherwise domain-specific languages like SQL to accomplish this task.

5.2: How to Manipulate/Transform Data?

The efficiency of analytical and business processes may be improved by data transformation, making it possible to make better decisions based on the data. The initial stage of the data transformation process should include activities such as converting the data type and flattening any hierarchical data. These actions format the data in a way that makes them more compatible with analytics tools. Data scientists and analysts can create additional transformations in an additive manner as required as specific levels of processing. Each layer of operations should be planned to carry out a distinct collection of responsibilities to fulfill a well-established business or technological need. Within the context of the data analytics stack, data transformation serves various purposes.

Parsing and Extraction

Data ingestion is the first step in the contemporary ELT process, starting with extracting information from such a data source. Next, the data is copied to where it will be stored. The first transformations concentrate on modifying the data's format and structure to make it compatible with the destination system and the already present data. One example of this kind of data transformation is extracting fields from log data that is comma delimited to put it into a relational database.

Mapping and Translating

Mapping and translating data are two of the most fundamental types of data transformations that may be performed.

For instance, if a column holding numbers that indicate error codes can be transferred to the necessary error descriptions, then that column will be much simpler to comprehend and more useful when shown in a program directed toward the end user.

Translating data involves converting it from one set of forms to another set of formats more suitable for the target system. Even after being parsed, the data from the website may come in the form that hierarchical JSON / XML files. These files need to be converted into column and row data before they can be included in the relational database.

Aggregating, Summarizing, and Filtering

The process of data transformation often involves paring down large amounts of data to make them more manageable. The filtering out of unneeded fields, columns, & records is required to condense the data. Records from business areas or numerical indexes in the data meant for graphs & dashboards may be examples of omitted data.

Additionally, specific research may not interest records from certain company regions.

Aggregating or summarizing the data is another possibility. Using techniques such as converting the time series of client interactions into daily or hourly sales figures, for example. Although BI systems can do these filtering and aggregating tasks, it is often more time and cost-effective to perform transformations on the data before the reporting tool sees the data.

Imputation and Enrichment of data

It is possible to develop denormalized and enhanced information by merging data from diverse sources. A client's transactions may be summed up into the total & added to a database that contains information about that customer to facilitate more rapid reference or use of customer analytics tools. Due to these changes, lengthy or freeform sections may be segmented into many columns. Additionally, missing values may be imputed, and damaged data may be replaced.

Sorting and Indexing

Data may be converted to be arranged logically or to conform to a data storage system to fulfill either of these purposes. Creating indexes, for instance, in relational management database systems may increase performance and facilitate the management of links between distinct databases.

Anonymization and Encryption

Data that contains personally identifiable information or other information that might compromise privacy or security should be anonymized before it is propagated. It is because such information could undermine privacy or security. It is necessary to encrypt sensitive information in many business sectors, and computer systems can carry out this function on various scales, from the level of individual database columns/cells to that of whole records and fields.

Modeling, Formatting, Typecasting, and Renaming

Finally, a whole suite of transformations may rearrange data without altering the substance of the records. It involves renaming tables, schemas, and columns for clarity, as well as casting & converting data types to ensure compatibility. Other tasks include altering dates and times using offsets and format translation and modifying dates and times.

5.3: Improving Data Transformation

Replicating the data in a data warehouse designed specifically for analytics is a prerequisite to running analytics at your company and even transforming the data in the first place. Most modern businesses choose a data warehouse hosted on the cloud, enabling them to fully use ELT. Stitch can put all the data into the data warehouse of your choice in an unprocessed state, ready to transform. Get a free trial of Stitch.

Users of Astera Centerprise(software name) may extract, map, convert, and load any data in a code-free atmosphere. It is a full-featured data integration platform. It also has features for other kinds of data transformation, such as data profiling capabilities, enabling customers to comprehensively understand their data. Additionally, you may profile data to contrast its prior and subsequent statistical summary.

Chapter 6: Working on Multiple Tables

6.1: Using JOINS For Multiple Tables

An SQL action known as a join is carried out to create a link among two or more databases by using columns from identical databases. It results in the establishment of a relationship between both tables. Most sophisticated queries in a SQL management system for databases use JOIN statements.

There are several varieties of joints to choose from. Which records the query selects on the kind of join the programmer chooses. Sort-merge joins, Hash join, & nested loop join are the three algorithms that act behind the scenes of join operations.

The inner join is the kind that is used by default. An inner join takes records from the second table and picks those that have values that match each other. Entries that do not include values that match or are common to other records are not included in the output. To locate rows that fulfill the join predicate, the query examines every row of the initial table in conjunction with records from the second table.

For example, if one data has employee information and another table contains manager information, it is possible to show employees that are also managers by performing a join on the employee or manager tables. It is because both tables have information about the respective roles.

A join operation is always carried out, and a query's "ON" phrase is where you specify which columns should be compared. The "Managerid" column is the one that matches this illustration. It is referred to as an equijoin since the operator "=" is utilized.

A normal join also produces the same output as the other join methods but includes the term "USING" in the join clause.

A join operation is carried out between the two tables regardless of whether a matched column is supplied. The simplest type of join is called a cross join, frequently referred to as a Cartesian product. This type of connection is known as the cross join. Due to the absence of a restriction on the key, every column in the initial table gets connected with every row inside the separate table. The output will contain six rows even though the first table has only two rows and the second one only has three.

Another essential sort of connector is known as the outer join. In general, outer joins include the input of all records from one table and the output from the other that matches those records. There are two possible configurations for an exterior join: a left outer connect or a right outer join. The output of a left external use of innovation contains all the tables that are part of the left table, regardless of whether they fulfill the matching constraints, as well as the rows from the right table that correspond to those tables. When doing a left outer join, the output will consist of every row from the right table and every matching row from the left table.

Several exceptional circumstances in which a table may be linked to itself. This kind of connection is known as a self-join.

It is essential to appreciate how to use JOINS in SQL Server. You'll often need to obtain and integrate data from several tables as you develop from a basic database user to a more experienced one. SQL Complete steps in to assist at this stage. Even for intricate JOIN statements, its code completion function performs effectively. Since dbForge SQL Comprehensive will recommend a whole JOIN clause using foreign keys or conditions based upon column names, you won't need to learn several column names or aliases. These options are displayed following the JOIN but On keywords.

More than that, when you join tables based upon foreign keys, SQL Complete may suggest a full SQL JOIN statement. You may manually choose a JOIN expression from the prompt list if you want a particular JOIN action.

6.2: Types of JOINS

SQL Server can support a wide variety of joins, some of which are referred to as "inner joins," "self joins," "cross joins," and "outer joins." The join type determines how two tables are connected in a query is determined LEFT OUTER JOINTS, RIGHT OUTER JOINTS, and FULL OUTER JOINTS are the three possible subcategories that may be applied to OUTER JOINTS.

- The result table for a SQL INNER JOIN query is created by joining records from multiple tables with identical values.
- The mismatched rows from the table supplied first before the LEFT OUTER JOIN phrase are added to the result table during the LEFT OUTER JOIN operation.
- The RIGHT OUTER JOIN operation generates a result table, and all the records from the right table and just the rows from the left table that match are included.
- SQL SELF JOIN enables you to compare rows inside the same

database by joining the table to itself.

- The CROSS-JOIN operation in SQL produces a result table that contains a paired mix of each row in the first table for each row in the second table for each row in both tables.

INNER JOIN

The INNER JOIN statement is used to get data in both tables and is responsible for returning just those entries or rows that include identical values.

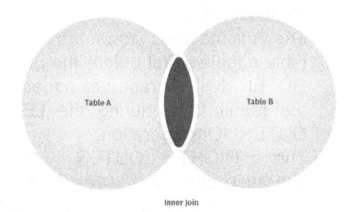

Inner Join

In this example, we wish to extract data from the Sales.SalesOrderDetail database as well as the Production. The product table is aliased with the letters

SOD and P, respectively. We are going to match entries in those columns using the JOIN statement. Take note of the process via which SQL Complete makes code recommendations.

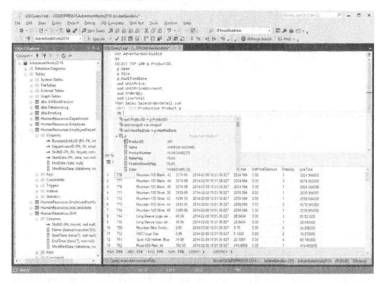

OUTER JOIN

When a SQL INNER JOIN is applied, the output will only provide results from the specified tables that fit the criteria. On the other hand, if you use a SQL OUTER JOIN, it will obtain the rows that match and retrieve the ones that do not match.

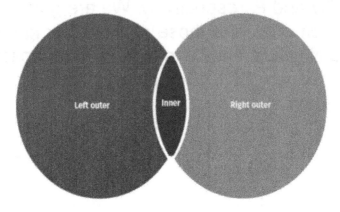

A result is returned using a FULL OUTER JOIN that incorporates data from both the left and the right tables. If no rows in the database correspond to the row inside the left table, all fields on the right side of the table will be empty. If there are no rows on the right side of the table that match the entry in the left table, then the corresponding column within the left table will still have nulls.

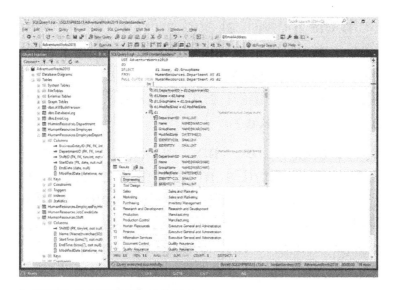

LEFT OUTER JOIN

The outcome of LEFT OUTER JOIN is comprised of rows identical to those in both tables. If no entries in the left table match, it displays those records as null values.

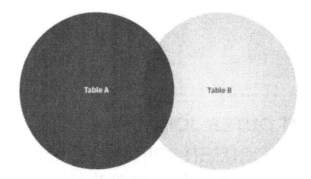

In the context of our example, we wish to link the tables under the heading Person.

Both the individual and human resources. The employee is used to obtain a list of each of the Persons' Last Names, but it also displays the Person's Job Title if they are an Employee.

If there are no workers whose BusinessEntityIDs match, the output will show rows with NULL values for NationalIDNumber or JobTitle. It will occur when no workers match the BusinessEntityID.

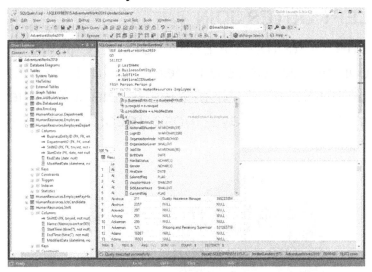

RIGHT OUTER JOIN

A RIGHT OUTER JOIN follows the same logic behind its operation as its counterpart, a LEFT OUTER JOIN. A RIGHT OUTER JOIN takes data from the right table, Table B, and uses it to find matching rows in the left table. A result set is returned by the RIGHT JOIN operation that contains all rows inside the right table, regardless of whether those rows match the left table. If a row inside the right side of the table does not match any corresponding rows as in the left table, the corresponding column in the result set for the left table will include nulls.

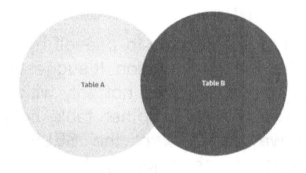

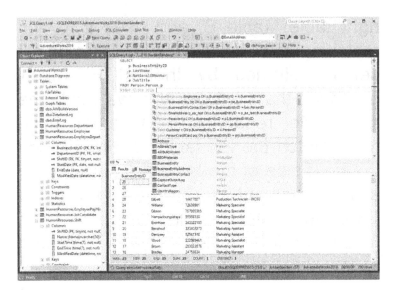

SELF JOIN

You may link a table to oneself by using the SELF JOIN operation. It suggests that each column is joined not only with itself but also with every other table column. One way to think of the SELF JOIN operation is as a joining between two different versions of a single table. SQL executes the instruction as if the table were being duplicated, even though this does not occur. It is performed by assigning a unique name to each copy of the table, which may be done with the help of table name aliases. The best applications for it involve extracting hierarchical data or comparing rows included in the same table.

In this example, we need to extract a list of all the salespeople working in each territory from the Sales.SalesPerson database.

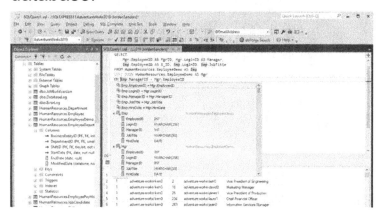

CROSS JOIN

When you use the CROSS-JOIN function in SQL, also known as just a cartesian join, the program will send back/return all possible combinations of entries from each table. Imagine that you must discover all possible sizes and color combinations of the item. In such a scenario, a CROSS JOIN may prove to be useful. Note that to link two tables together, this join is not required for any conditions to be met. CROSS JOIN syndicates every row after the first table through every row since the distinct table, and the result includes all possible combinations of records from the first and second tables.

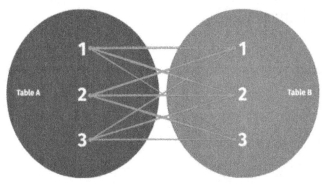

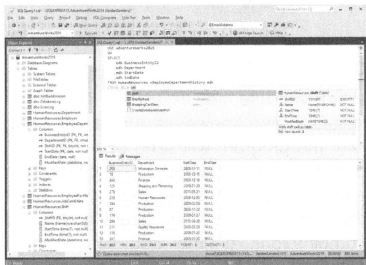

6.3: Advantages of JOINS

With JOINS, you may precisely get the data you need from any of the tables with a single query, using whatever search criteria you want to filter your results. It is made possible because you only need to use one query. Your API code cannot use performance-enhancing features such as indexes, but MySQL can do so.

Executing many searches and using some application programming interface (API), such as PHP, to screen the results often results in additional overhead for servers. In addition to the fact that MySQL was designed for maximum efficiency, which cannot be guaranteed while working with per-developer API code, the amount of data that must be transmitted back and forth between MySQL and the API has significantly increased.

The utilization of joins comes with an additional set of benefits. You will be able to increase the amount of the calculating weight placed on the database if you use rather than several queries. It indicates that you will be able to make greater use of the capabilities of the database, such as its capability to search through, limit, sort, etc.

Here is an illustration: Consider for a moment that you need to search for information in several distinct tables. You may do this by utilizing table joins in a single query, or you could do it in numerous queries, and then you can package it data for presentation using something like PHP. But let's assume you're interested in "paginating." Let's imagine you don't want to extract every row that satisfies your pick criteria all at once, but rather only a small number of them, say 25 at a time. And let's assume you want to remove the "three page" of this selection, sometimes known as rows 51 to 75. What would this look like? You can perform this choice very easily by using the limit phrase "limit 51,25" if we configure this to utilize just one query instead of many queries that employ table joins. By doing it in this manner, you will extract the 25 columns that you desire and nothing more.

If you chose to do this with query keywords instead, you would have to effectively extract all the rows that matched all the queries, perform any necessary manipulations in PHP arrays afterward, and then throw away everything except for the 25 rows that you want to show. If you did this, you could then display the rows. You cannot just apply the "limit 51,25" condition on each query since the row positions of the results from each query will not, in most cases, be the same.

In most cases, it is in everyone's best interest to move as many calculations relating to the selection into the database as possible. If, on the other hand, the query that is generated is excessively intricate and leads to an excessive amount of computing work on the part of the database (and adding some few indices does not assist), then it is preferable to divide the job down into many inquiries and complete it that way.

Chapter 7 Functions

Utilizing and modifying data to develop insights that may assist organizations in solving an issue or discovering possibilities is what the term "data analysis " means. "It doesn't worry how skilled you are at constructing intricate models or creating fancy visualizations if you can't get beyond the fact that you need statistics to perform those things as a network engineer or data scientist. When working for a major corporation, these records are often entered into a database where they can be queried and easily accessed by everyone.

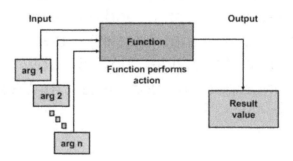

It makes it possible for everyone to perform their jobs effectively. Anyone who engages in the data analysis process might be considered a data analyst. Many businesses use the term "data analyst" as a professional job title. Cleaning and manipulating data, modeling it in certain formats, and developing visualizations or views to emphasize knowledge that decision-makers can access are some of the thus as of a data analyst. Recently, attendance has been a major uptick in the availability of well-paying positions in data analysis. However, regardless of the job description, many employees engage in data analysis as part of their regular work. Learning skills typical of data analysts, such as SQL, is extremely beneficial for almost anyone who takes the time to do so.

Pretend that you have just launched a new internet-based business where you offer rare and unusual teas to customers worldwide. Within the first year of your company's existence, you have built up a customer base of one hundred thousand people and made sales of one million dollars' worth of goods. That looks like a good place to get started. Nevertheless, you aim to scale up to ten million dollars in revenue during the next 2 years.

Increasing the number of individuals who purchase your goods or selling more to the people you already have are the two primary ways a business can boost its sales. Let's imagine that the first thing you want to do is increase the number of orders coming from your existing pool of customers. You currently have 100,000 customers, and each order was for an average of ten dollars. One strategy for increasing revenue from existing customers is encouraging them to purchase additional kinds of tea. You can still use SQL to start grouping your consumers into categories determined by their purchases, also known as segments. Suppose you want to separate your consumers into two categories: Loyalists purchase only one to three different kinds of tea. Customers of Variety Shops purchase more than three different kinds of tea. The objective is to get the Variety of Shoppers interested in new products so that you may either 1) enable a high prevalence of orders for various things or 2) produce more value per transaction from much more items in customers' carts. You might offer

Loyalists deals on similar products based on the quantity they buy. When I say, "quantity bargains," I'm referring to discounts and freebies that customers can get if they buy more of the exact item.

7.1: Functions

SQLite-based applications can construct their custom SQL functions, then call back into the existing applications to compute the results. It is possible to incorporate the implementations of the custom SQL functions into the application code directly, or they might be loadable extensions instead. Using the sqlite3 create function() family of interfaces, application-defined, custom SQL functions can be crafted. Scalar values, aggregate functions, and window functions are the three types of custom SQL functions you can use. The highest number of reasons that can be passed to a custom SQL function is defined by the constant SQLITE MAX FUNCTION ARG. The callbacks executed to carry out a process for the basic SQL function are specified by the sqlite3 create function()

interface. SQLite supports custom table-valued functions; however, SQLite uses a different methodology to implement them, and that method will not be discussed in this document.

7.2: Brand-New Functions

To develop new custom SQL functions, the sqlite3 create function() set of interfaces is utilized. Everyone in this family serves as a covering for a fundamental component in common all of them. Everyone in the family contributes to the same goal; their calling cards only have various names.

1. sqlite3 create function()

The initial version of sqlite3 create function() allows the software to create a separate new SQL function. This new SQL function can be either a vector quantity or an aggregate. The UTF8 encoding is used to specify the identifier of the function.

2. sqlite3 create function16()

The key/only difference between this version & the original sqlite3 create function() is that the identifier of the service itself is supplied as a UTF16 text rather than a UTF8 string. Other than that, the functionality is the same.

3. sqlite3 create function v2()

This option/variant operates in the same manner as the original sqlite3 create function(), with the exception that it contains an additional parameter in the form of a pointer to a null pointer for the sqlite3 user data() pointer. This pointer is passed as the 5th debate to all the sqlite3 create function() variants. This destructor function is called when the bespoke function is removed, often when the DB connection is closed. It happens only if the destructor function is not NULL. sqlite3 create window function() is referred to as "sqlite3." This variant performs the same functions as the original sqlite3 create function(), except that it receives a separate set of callback pointers, specifically the callback pointers used by glass function definitions.

7.3: Parameters

The sqlite3 create function(a) variety of interfaces shares many of its parameters with other members of its own family. Many of these parameters are called "common." DB, the first parameter of a custom SQL function, is almost always a reference to the MySQL database on which it will operate. Each database connection requires its own unique set of individualized custom SQL routines to be developed. There is no convenient technique for building SQL functions compatible with all database connections that can be used as a shorthand.

zFunctionName

It is the identity of the SQL function, which is being generated, and it is the second parameter in this command. The name is typically encoded in UTF8, except that the name for sqlite3 create function16 must be encoded in UTF16 inside this native byte order (). The height of a SQL given function can be no longer than 255 UTF8 bytes at most. An SQLite MISUSE error will be generated whenever it is attempted to define a method with a name that is longer. There is no threshold on the number of times a SQL function creation endpoint can be called using the same data type.

For instance, if two requests have the same method number but a variable number of arguments, then two variations of the SQL procedure will also be registered, each of which will take a different set of arguments. The quantity of arguments such a function is willing to take is indicated by the third parameter, which is always referred to as nArg.

The value needs to be an integer that falls something between -1 and SQLITE MAX FUNCTION ARG. If a SQL function has a value of -1, it indicates that it is a variadic function, which means it can handle any number of parameters from 0 to SQLITE MAX FUNCTION ARG.

eTextRep

The fourth parameter seems to be a 32-bit integer flag. The bits of this flag communicate various characteristics regarding the new function. The initial role of this argument was to provide the text encoding that the function preferred to use. It could be done by selecting one of the constants, including SQLite UTF8, SQLITE UTF16BE and SQLITE UTF16LE. Text in any encoding can be passed through any custom SQL function. All necessary encoding conversions will be performed mechanically. The only purpose served by the preferred encoding is to specify the encoding about which the function is optimized. Configuring diverse uses with the same name and the exact percentage of arguments is possible, but different encodings and unique callbacks were used to implement the function. SQLite will choose the set of callbacks that require the input encodings greatest closely match the favored encoding. It can be done by specifying diverse uses with identical names and the exact number . of arguments. Recently, additional flag bits have been added to the 4th argument to communicate additional information regarding the function. The additional components include SQLite DETERMINISTIC, SQLITE DIRECTONLY, SQLITE INNOCUOUS and SQLITE SUBTYPE.

There is a possibility that additional bytes will be included in subsequent editions of SQLite. The Papp is a subjective link to the recall/callback routines, and the fifth parameter seems to be an arbitrary pointer. The only thing that SQLite does with a pointer makes it accessible to callbacks and then send it to the destructor when a function is unregistered. Other than that, it does nothing with it. Invoking sqlite3 create function() numerous times for the very same SQL function is normal practice for applications. For instance, if a SQL function may accept two or three parameters, then sqlite3 create function() would be executed once for the two-argument version and again for the three-argument version. The fundamental implementation, called callbacks, may be distinct for each version. In addition, an application may register numerous SQL processes with the same name, the same number of parameters, and a different text encoding for each of those procedures. In that instance, SQLite will invoke its function by utilizing the hooks for the version of SQLite whose preference text encoding is the one that corresponds to the text encoding of the database the most precisely. This approach will likely provide numerous representations of the same function, each optimized for either UTF8 or UTF16. If countless calls to sqlite3 create function() specify the same function name, the same number of reasoning, and the same favorite text encoding, therefore the callbacks and some other variables of the third message overwrite those of the first call, and the memory allocator callback from the original call (if it persists) is invoked. It happens if multiple demands to sqlite3 create function() specify the same function name.

Chapter 8: Subqueries

When we mix different facts, dimensions, and data sources, we may gain new insights from relational databases, leading to significant value in data science. In this chapter, we will define subqueries, discuss their benefits and drawbacks, and how they assist us in merging data from several tables.

8.1 What are subqueries?

The term "subqueries" refers to inquiries included inside other queries. Storing data in additional than one table is common when interacting with a relational database.

Subqueries may be used to combine data from various sources into a single table, and they can also assist with adding additional filtering criteria to a query.

If we want to know all the customers who have an order having freight exceeding 100, that would be an example of a subquery. The information about the freight is stored in one record, and the information about the customers is stored in another table. A SQL query enclosed/nested inside another query is known as a subquery. The SELECT clause is one place where The subquery may appear in the following.

- SELECT clause
- FROM statement
- WHERE clause

A subquery may be nested(fully contained) inside another subquery or a SELECT, UPDATE, INSERT or DELETE statement. Typically, a subquery is appended to a different SQL SELECT statement's WHERE clause. Comparison operators like > or = may be used. A multiple-row operator, these as IN, ANY, or ALL, can also be used as the comparison operator. The statement comprising a subquery is referred to as an outer or outer query, while a subquery is referred to as an inner or inner query. The inner query runs it before the parent query, for the outer query may use the inner query's results.

The following actions may be carried out using a subquery in the

SELECT, DELETE, INSERT, or UPDATE statement:

- Evaluate an expression against the query's result.
- Check to see whether the results of the query contain an expression.
- Verify if the query selects any rows.

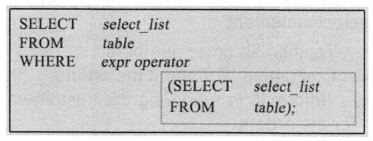

8.2 Best Practices for Subquery

In this part, we'll go over several recommended practices for using subqueries, including the following

- Instructions on how to compose subqueries inside subqueries
- The excessive usage of subqueries causes several performance issues.
- How to do computations using subqueries

Although there is no superior/upper limit to the number of subqueries you may use, the efficiency of your query will suffer if you nest it too deeply. Keep in mind/attention that it is only possible to get a single column using subquery selections.

Multiple levels of nested subqueries

An example of the subquery inside a subquery can be seen in the following select statement

- Toothbrush order numbers
- Customers IDS about the orders
- Information regarding the customers for the orders

8.3: Guidelines for Subqueries

When working with subqueries, there are a few best practices to keep in mind:

- A parenthetical expression is required around a subquery.
- On the comparison operator's right-hand side, a subquery must be put.
- Since subqueries cannot change their results on the fly, it is impossible to include an ORDER BY clause inside a subquery. In the main SELECT statement, also known as the outer query, you can include an ORDER BY clause as the statement's last clause.

- When working with single-row subqueries, use single-row operators.
- When utilizing certain comparison operators in a WHERE clause, an outer query would not return any rows if a subquery (inner query) provides a null result to the outer query.

8.4: Various Types of Subqueries

- Returns either zero(0) or one(1) row when using a single row subquery.
- Multiple column subqueries: Returns one or maybe more columns.
- Returns more rows or one row and may return several rows if necessary.
- Sub questions related: Make a reference to one or more columns within a statement surrounding the inner one. Because of its connection to the parent SQL expression, the subquery in question is sometimes referred to by the term "correlated subquery."
- Subqueries inside subqueries: It is common practice to nest one subquery inside another.

8.5: Correlated subqueries

It is possible to evaluate/analyze many queries by just running the subquery once & then inserting the value or values that were returned from that execution into the WHERE clause of the larger query. When conducting searches that contain a correlated subquery, also known as a recurring subquery, the values returned by the subquery depend on the results of the primary query. It indicates that the subquery is carried out several times for every row that the outer query has the potential to pick. This query will retrieve one instance from each employee's initial and last name for those employees whose bonus inside the SalesPerson table is 5000 & whose employee identification figures match in the Employee table and the SalesPerson table. Additionally, this query will retrieve one specific case of each employee's bonus in the SalesPerson table.

Table-valued functions may also be included in the FROM clause of correlated subqueries, which is accomplished by referring to columns from a table with an outer query as a parameter of the table-valued function. In this instance, the table-valued function gets evaluated per the subquery for each row returned by the outer query.

8.6: Comparison operators in subqueries

One of the comparison operators (=, >, >, > =,! >, or!) may be used to initiate the construction of a subquery. When a subquery is launched using an unmodified comparison operator, a comparison operator not preceded by ANY or ALL, the subquery is required to return a single result rather than a list of values, as is the case with subqueries beginning with IN. If this subquery produces several results, SQL Server will generate an error message.

To employ a subquery that is introduced with an unaltered comparison operator, you need to have sufficient knowledge of both your data and the nature of the issue to determine that the subquery may return precisely one response. You can write a statement that contains a subquery that is introduced with a simple = comparison operator if, for instance, you assume that each salesperson is only responsible for one sales territory, and you want to discover the customers that are in the territory that Linda Mitchell covers.

```
USE AdventureWorks2016;
GO
SELECT CustomerID
FROM Sales.Customer
WHERE TerritoryID =
    (SELECT TerritoryID
     FROM Sales.SalesPerson
     WHERE BusinessEntityID = 276);
GO
```

On the other hand, an error warning would be generated if Linda Mitchell covered over one sales region simultaneously. An IN formulation might be used as the comparison operator instead of =, or =ANY could be used instead. The employment of aggregate functions in subqueries introduced with unaltered comparison operators is common since these operators only return a single result. For instance, the statement below discovers the names of all items whose list price is higher than the average list price for all products in the category.

```
USE AdventureWorks2016;
GO
SELECT [Name]
FROM Production.Product
WHERE ListPrice >
    (SELECT AVG (ListPrice)
     FROM Production.Product);
GO
```

Because subqueries started with unaltered comparison operators are required to yield a single result, you cannot put GROUP BY / HAVING clauses in them unless you are certain the clauses themselves return a single value. For instance, the following query locates all the goods in ProductSubcategoryID 14 with prices greater than the category's item with the lowest price.

```
USE AdventureWorks2016;
GO
SELECT [Name]
FROM Production.Product
WHERE ListPrice >
    (SELECT MIN (ListPrice)
     FROM Production.Product
     GROUP BY ProductSubcategoryID
     HAVING ProductSubcategoryID = 14);
GO
```

Chapter 9: Views

The data organization in relational databases is accomplished using various database objects, such as tables, stored procedures, views, clusters, etc. Organizing tables inside a database to cut down on duplication and dependence in a SQL database is a recommended best practice. Normalization is a procedure that occurs inside a database to organize the data that is stored within the database by dividing huge tables into many smaller tables. The use of the relationships connects these few tables. To access data from different databases and fields, developers build queries. We may utilize many joins in the query, which may cause the query to become too convoluted and difficult to comprehend. To get the data, users should additionally be required to have rights to the objects.

In SQL, views may be thought of as "virtual tables." Rows and columns are likewise present in a view, just as they are in an actual table in the database. We can create a view by picking out fields from any or all the tables included inside the database. A View may include all the rows of the table or just the rows that satisfy the given criteria for a subset of those rows.

9.1: Creating a SQL VIEW

The following syntax should be used to create a VIEW

Code

CREATE VIEW Name AS

Select col1, col2...coln From tables

Where conditions.

Example 1: Using SQL VIEW to get each entry from a database

It is the simplest form of VIEW. Usually, we do not utilize a VIEW in SQL Server to fetch all records from a single table.

Code

CREATE VIEW EmployeeRecord

AS

    SELECT *

    FROM   [HumanResource].

[Employee];

You may access a VIEW the same way you would a SQL table after it has been built.

Example 2: Using SQL VIEW, get a few database columns

Not all the columns in a table may be of interest to us. Within the select statement, we can define the column names necessary to get just those fields from the database.

Code

```
CREATE VIEW EmployeeRecord
AS
    SELECT
NIDNumber,LoginID,JobTitle
    FROM                [HumanResource].
[Employee];
```

Example 3: Using the WHERE clause, a SQL VIEW may be used to get a table's first few columns

Through the usage of a Where clause conditional in a Select statement, we can filter the results.

Let's say we need to get EmployeeRecords with the marital status 'M.'

Code

```
CREATE VIEW EmployeeRecord
AS
    SELECT NIDNumber,
       LoginID,
       JobTitle,
       MarriedStatus
    FROM [HumanResource].[Employee]
    WHERE MarriedStatus = 'M';
```

Example 4: Using SQL VIEW to get data from many different tables

We can select a line with Join conditions between many tables using the VIEW command. It is a common example of how a VIEW may be used in SQL Server. In the send-a-follow, we employ INNER JOIN with LEFT OUTER JOIN across different tables to get a few fields per our specifications.

Code

```
CREATE VIEW [Sales].[vStoreContacts]
AS
    SELECT s.[BusinessEntityID],
        s.[Name],
        ct.[Name] AS [Contact_Type],
        p.[Title],
        p.[First_Name],
        p.[Middle_Name],
        p.[Last_Name],
        p.[Suffix],
        pp.[Number],
        ea.[Email],
        p.[Email_Promotion]
    FROM [Sales].[Store] s
        INNER JOIN [Person].[BusinessEntityContact] bec ON bec.[BusinessEntityID] = s.[BusinessEntityID]
        INNER JOIN [Person].[Contact_Type] ct ON ct.[ContactTypeID] = bec.[ContactTypeID]
        INNER JOIN [Person].[Person] p ON p.[BusinessEntityID] = bec.[PersonID]
        LEFT OUTER JOIN [Person].[Email] ea ON ea.[BusinessEntityID] = p.[BusinessEntityID]
        LEFT OUTER JOIN [Person].[PPhone] pp ON pp.[BusinessEntityID] = p.[BusinessEntityID];
GO
```

Imagine/Consider that you must run this query extremely regularly. We need to write one line of code to get the data using a VIEW.

Code

select * from [Sales].[vStoreContacts]

	BusinessEntityID	Name	ContactType	Title	FirstName	MiddleName	LastName
1	292	Next-Door Bike Store	Owner	Mr.	Gustavo	NULL	Achong
2	294	Professional Sales and Service	Owner	Ms.	Catherine	R.	Abel
3	296	Riders Company	Owner	Ms.	Kim	NULL	Abercrombie
4	298	The Bike Mechanics	Owner	Sr.	Humberto	NULL	Acevedo
5	300	Nationwide Supply	Owner	Sra.	Pilar	NULL	Ackerman
6	302	Area Bike Accessories	Owner	Ms.	Frances	B.	Adams
7	304	Bicycle Accessories and Kits	Owner	Ms.	Margaret	J.	Smith
8	306	Clamps & Brackets Co.	Owner	Ms.	Carla	J.	Adams
9	316	Fun Toys and Bikes	Owner	Mr.	Robert	E.	Ahlering
10	318	Great Bikes	Owner	Mr.	François	NULL	Ferrier
11	320	Metropolitan Sales and Rental	Owner	Ms.	Kim	NULL	Akers

Example 5: Use SQL VIEW to get a certain column

In the last example, we generated a VIEW by combining many tables and selecting a few columns from each of those tables. Once we have created a view, getting each column included inside the view is unnecessary. A VIEW with SQL Server that is analogous to a related table allows us to pick a limited number of columns.

In the send-a-follow, we are just interested in retrieving two columns from the view: the Name and the contract type.

Code

```
SELECT Name,
      Contact_Type
FROM [Sales].[vStoreContacts];
```

Example 6: You may obtain the VIEW definition by using Sp help text

We may take advantage of the system stored method sp help text get the definition of VIEW. It gives back a comprehensive explanation of what a SQL VIEW is.

Let's take an example and look at the definition of the view called EmployeeRecords VIEW.

```
Text
-----------------------------------------------------------------
CREATE VIEW EmployeeRecords
AS                                    Sp_helptext 'EmployeeRecords'
    SELECT NationalIDNumber,
           LoginID,
           JobTitle,
           MaritalStatus
    FROM [HumanResources].[Employee]
    WHERE MaritalStatus = 'M';
```

We may also utilize SSMS as an alternative to producing the code for a VIEW. Expand the database, click Views, right-click and go to the Script view as a menu option, click Create Too, and finally choose New Query Builder Window.

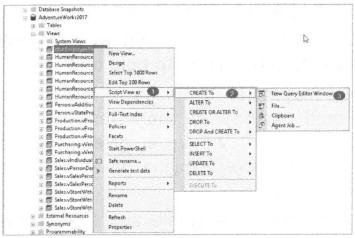

Example 7: sp_refreshview is a utility for refreshing a SQL VIEW's metadata.

Let's say we have a VIEW built on top of a table that uses the select * statement for extracting all the columns from that data.

Code

CREATE VIEW DemoView

AS

SELECT *

FROM [AdventureWorks2017].[dbo].[MyTable];

The following is the output provided after we have called the VIEW DemoView.

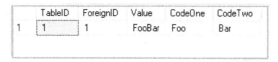

Let's use the Alter table command to include a new column inside the table.

Code

Alter Table [AdventureWorks2017].[dbo].[MyTable] Add City varchar(50)

You will need to rerun the select statement to get records from VIEW. In addition to that, the new column needs to be shown in the output. The output has not changed at all and does not include the column that was only recently introduced.

	TableID	ForeignID	Value	CodeOne	CodeTwo
1	1	1	FooBar	Foo	Bar

The schema or metadata associated with the VIEW is not altered by default when using SQL Server. To update any view's information, we may use the system saved procedure known as sp refreshview.

Code

Exec sp_refreshview DemoView

You will need to rerun the select statement to get records from VIEW. Within the output, the City column is visible to us.

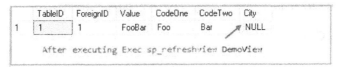

After executing Exec sp_refreshview DemoView

Example 8: Binding the Schema of a SQL View

In the preceding example, we made some changes to the SQL database to create a new field. Imagine that you are operating in the production environment and have access to a view of the program. You are not informed of the modifications made to the table's design to accommodate the additional column. It is important that the VIEW not be updated with any changes to the tables it uses. We can use the SCHEMABINDING parameter to lock all the tables used in this VIEW and prevent any edit table statements from being executed against those tables.

Let's put the following query to the test and include an option. SCHEMA BINDING.

Code

```
CREATE VIEW DemoView
WITH SCHEMA BINDING
AS
    SELECT *
    FROM   [AdventureWorks2017].[dbo].[MyTable];
```

It produces an error message.

We cannot call all columns within a VIEW that uses the SCHEMABINDING option (Select *). Let's run the following query again once we have specified the columns to include in it.

Code

CREATE VIEW DemoView

WITH SCHEMA BINDING

AS

SELECT TableID, ForeignID ,Value, codeine

FROM [AdventureWorks2017].[dbo].[MyTable];

Once again, the next error message is shown.

Within my query, I used a three-part unique identifier following the style [DBName.Schema.Object]. This format is incompatible with the SCHEMABINDING parameter in a VIEW. Thus we cannot use it. According to the following query, we can utilize the two-part Name.

Code

```
CREATE VIEW DemoView
WITH SCHEMA BINDING
AS
    SELECT TableID, ForeignID ,Value, CodeOne
    FROM [dbo].[MyTable];
|
```

After you have produced a VIEW using the SCHEMABINDING option, use the Alter table command to experiment with adding or modifying the data type of a column.

```
ALTER TABLE dbo.MyTable ALTER COLUMN ForeignID BIGINT;
```

```
Msg 5074, Level 16, State 1, Line 12
The object 'DemoView' is dependent on column 'ForeignID'.
Msg 4922, Level 16, State 9, Line 12
ALTER TABLE ALTER COLUMN ForeignID failed because one or more objects access this column.
```

Before we can make any changes to the already defined schema of the table, we need to remove the VIEW meaning itself and any other dependencies upon the table.

Example 8: SQL VIEW ENCRYPTION

With the WITH ENCRYPTION clause, we can encrypt the VIEW. Previously, we used the sp help text command to determine whether users could access the view definition. We have the option of encrypting the definition if we do not desire people to be able to read it.

Code

```
CREATE VIEW DemoView
WITH ENCRYPTION
AS
    SELECT TableID, ForeignID ,Value, CodeOne
    FROM [dbo].[MyTable];
```

When you try to examine the definition by using the sp help text command at this time, you will get the following error.

Code

Exec sp_helptext DemoView

The text associated with the item "DemoView" has been encrypted.

Example 9: SQL VIEW for DML queries

We may utilize SQL VIEW to add, update and remove data from a single Database table. Only one table at a time is eligible for DML operations from our side.

- It is not appropriate for VIEW to include the Group By, Having, or Distinct clauses.
- In SQL Server, we cannot utilize a subquery inside a VIEW.
- In a SQL VIEW, we are unable to utilize the Set operator.

Use the following queries to perform a DML action using VIEW in SQL Server.

- Insert DML - Insert into DemoView values(4,'CC','KK','RR')
- Delete DML - Delete from DemoView where TableID=7

- Update DML - Update DemoView set value='Raj' where TableID=5

Example 10: VIEW and the Check Option in SQL

With the WITH CHECK option, we can determine whether the VIEW criteria correspond to the DML statements.

It stops rows from being inserted into the table in cases when the criterion specified in its Where clause also isn't met.

If the condition is not met, an error message will be generated in either the insert or update statement.

In the end, we use the CHECK option, and in the [Codeone] column, we wish to restrict the values to those that begin with the letter F.

Code

```
CREATE VIEW DemoView
AS
    SELECT *
    FROM [dbo].[MyTable]
    WHERE [Codeone] LIKE 'F%'
WITH THE CHECK OPTION;
```

The next error message will be displayed on our screen if we attempt to input a value that doesn't satisfy the criterion.

Insert into DemoView values (5,'CC','Raj','Raj')

```
Msg 550, Level 16, State 1, Line 1
The attempted insert or update failed because the target view either specifies
WITH CHECK OPTION or spans a view that specifies WITH CHECK OPTION and one or more rows
resulting from the operation did not qualify under the CHECK OPTION constraint.
The statement has been terminated.
```

Example 11: Dropping SQL VIEW

Utilizing the DROP VIEW command, we can drop a view. Within the send-a-follow, we wish to get rid of the VIEW demo view stored in SQL Server.

Code

DROP VIEW demo view;

Example 12: Altering a SQL VIEW

Using the below alter VIEW command, we can modify the SQL statement included inside a VIEW. Let's say we want to modify the condition included in the where phrase of a VIEW. Carry out the inquiry that is listed below.

Code

```
Alter VIEW DemoView
AS
    SELECT *
    FROM [dbo].[MyTable]
    WHERE [Codeone] LIKE 'C%'
WITH THE CHECK OPTION;
```

With the announcement of Service Pack 1 for SQL Server 2016, it is possible to use the Construct or ALTER command to either build a SQL VIEW from scratch or alter an existing one.

Before the SQL Server 2016 Service Pack 1, we could not utilize CREATE and Alter simultaneously.

Code

```
CREATE OR ALTER VIEW DemoView
AS SELECT *
    FROM [dbo].[MyTable]
    WHERE [Codeone] LIKE 'C%'
WITH THE CHECK OPTION;
```

9.2: Advantages of View

Security

A user's accessibility to stored data may be restricted by allowing them to view the data only via a limited number of views that include the precise data they are permitted to see.

Query Simplicity

Multi-table queries against a view become single-table queries because the view may combine data from several tables into a single table and display it.

Structured brevity

By displaying a database as a collection of virtual columns which make sense to the user, views may provide a "personalized" view of a database schema to the user.

Consistency

Even if the application's source tables are divided, reorganized, or given new names, a view may still display a coherent, unaltered representation of the database's structure.

Data Reliability

The DBMS may automatically examine the data to ensure it complies with the given integrity requirements if it is accessed or entered via a view.

Impartial data in logic

The database and application tables may become somewhat autonomous thanks to views. The application should be based on the table if there isn't a view. With the help of the view, the program may be set up in the context of the previous view, allowing the program and a database column to be separated.

9.3: Disadvantages of View

Performance

The DBMS still must translate queries against a view into questions against the application's source tables even though views have the table's appearance. Simple queries on views may take a long time if a complicated, multi-table query specifies the view.

Update limitations

The DBMS must convert a user's request to update rows of a view into a change on rows of underlying source tables. Simple views can do this, but more complicated views are often read-only.

Chapter 10: Data Manipulation Language

SQL (in all its variants) as a command for constructing user-friendly dashboards and reporting tools is referred to as SQL for big data. SQL is likely the most common use of SQL in the modern day. SQL makes it possible to create user-friendly dashboards that can present information in various formats because of its ease of use in communicating complex commands to databases and its ability to change data in a matter of seconds. In addition, SQL is a good tool for building data warehouses since it is easy to access, clearly organized, and can communicate effectively. Another way that many people use SQL data analytics is by directly integrating them into other frameworks. It provides extra functionality and communication capabilities without the need to develop entire structures from the ground up. SQL analytics may be utilized within programming languages such as Scala, Python, and Hadoop.

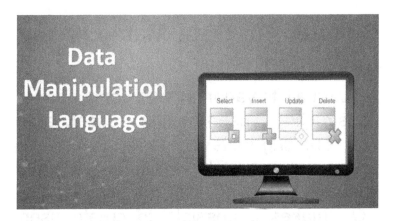

Data Manipulation Language

Select · Insert · Update · Delete

These are 3(three) of the most prominent programming languages that are now in use for data science & the management and processing of large amounts of data. Because SQL can interact directly with databases constructed in these languages, it can be used as a mediator between end users and a more complicated computer storage system that will be more accessible to experts and data scientists. It is because of SQL's ability to interact with datasets built in these languages. SQL, which is a database querying language, can interact with several databases at the same time, and it makes use of database systems. This capacity is referred to as SQL for data analysis. SQL was among the most widely used and versatile programming languages because it mixes a surprisingly easy period of adjustment with a complicated depth that enables users to construct sophisticated tools and panels for data analysis. It makes SQL one of the most popular programming languages. SQL has been modified into various private tools, each with its specialty and niche industry, including popular MySQL, Oracle Database, or PostgreSQL. The goal of these instruments/tools is to make it easier to quickly construct and interact with databases. SQL is widely used not only because it's a simple language but also because it can do surprisingly complicated data analysis. Its speed in creating databases and interacting with them continues to be the primary reason for its widespread use. The logic built into the language and the manner it communicates with data sources are quite like that of other programs such as Excel and the widely used Python module Pandas. DML is designed to resemble plain English and improve the user's ability to communicate effectively with the system.

The operational capabilities of DML are structured in manipulation commands such as SELECT, UPDATE, INSERT INTO, and DELETE FROM.

In retrieving rows from a table, you can use the SELECT statement. The format of the query is as follows: SELECT [field name(s)] from [student table] where [conditions]. The SELECT command is SQL's most popular and commonly used DML command.

UPDATE is a command that changes the data of one or even more records. UPDATE [table title] SET [col name = value] where [conditions] is an example of the syntax for an update command.

Adding one or more entries to a data store is the job of the INSERT command. INSERT INTO [table title] [column(s)] is the format for the insert command syntax. VALUES [value(s)].

DELETE is a command that, when executed, removes one record or more from a table based on the conditions that you specify. DELETE FROM [table] WHERE [condition] is the command syntax for deleting data.

Meaning of "Data Manipulation" The process of altering or manipulating information to make it more readable and organized is called "manipulation of data." To attain this goal, we make use of DML. What exactly does "DML" stand for? "DML" refers to "Data Manipulation Language," a programming language used to create, delete, and modify databases. It means that the information can be transformed into a form that can be read. Because DML is available, we can clean and structure the data to make it more easily edible for expression.

Modifying information to make it simpler to understand or more structured is known as "data manipulation." For instance, a data log could be sorted in alphabetical order, making it much simpler to discover certain entries inside the record. Data manipulation can also be applied to the web server logs to allow website owners to monitor its most popular pages and the traffic sources that lead to those pages. Users of accounting software or professionals in related industries may also modify data to evaluate the cost of production, pricing patterns, or potential tax liabilities. Data manipulation is another tool that stock market analysts employ to foresee movements in the stock exchange and how stocks will perform soon. Data manipulation is another method that computers can use to present information to consumers in a manner that is truer to life. The code drives this method in a viewer software programmer, web page, or document formatting. The alteration of data is only possible if you already possess the necessary information. Because of this, you require a database constructed from various data sources. Restructuring and rearrangement are required for this body of information. Your information can be made more accurate by the manipulation of data. Import a database, and then build a copy specifically for your use. Through the process of data manipulation, it is possible to combine, delete, or integrate information. The process of data analysis is simplified when the data are manipulated.

10.1: Purpose Of Data Manipulations

Data manipulation is an essential component of effective corporate operations and optimization. To use data effectively and transform it into useful information, such as through analyzing financial data, consumer behavior, and trends, you need to have the ability to work with the data in the way that you require it to be dealt with. Consequently, the manipulation of data confers several benefits upon an organization, such as the following

Consistent data

If you provide the information in a consistent format, it will be easier to structure, understand, and comprehend. When you take data from various sources, you may not get a unified picture of the data, but with falsification and procedures, you can ensure that the information is saved consistently and structured appropriately.

Data for projects

It is of the utmost significance for businesses to utilize past data to make predictions and give more in-depth analyses, particularly regarding financial matters. The manipulation of data is what makes it possible to achieve this goal.

When it comes to using data, having the capability to convert it, update it, remove it, and include it into a database all indicate that you have more options. - Develop further insights based on the data. When data is provided that does not change, it defeats its purpose. When you understand how to use data to your advantage, you will gain clear insights to make speedier business decisions. Erase or ignore superfluous data: material that cannot be used is constantly present and might get in the way of what matters. When you first glance at Data Manipulation Language, it has an awkward and unnatural appearance. For instance, describing to other people how to utilize a built-in functionality in Access is quite simple compared to describing to them how to use Late-night talk to Pick * FROM. However, DML is not a language that can be used for programming. That an implicit program can be understood by a computer and carried out by the machine cannot be built, nor can it be turned into 0s and 1s. Instead, think of it as a complex formula that one could see in a spreadsheet. When you work with a spreadsheet, you presumably use some complicated formulas. DML is simply formula-speak for referring to the process of working with a database. Suppose you are interested in beginning to work with data manipulation. In that case, the following are the steps you need to consider: The alteration of data is only possible if you already possess the necessary information. Because of this, you require a database constructed from various data sources. Restructuring and rearrangement are required for this body of information. Your information can be made more accurate by the manipulation of data. Import a database, and then build a copy specifically for your use. Through the process of data manipulation, it is possible to combine, delete, or integrate information. The process of data analysis is simplified when the data are manipulated.

Columns and formulas are helpful up to a certain point when working with data held in a database using SQL; however, there comes the point where you want to do some intricate data interactions, and you can no longer rely on tables and formulas. In a circumstance like that, you will most likely require Data Manipulation Vocabulary. The Data Manipulation Language (DML) is a technique to communicate with a database in a format designed from the ground up to be understood by the system. This format allows you to tell the database exactly what you want it to do.

When performing operations within existing data, such as adding, transferring, or erasing data, the Data Manipulation Vocabulary provides an effective and efficient method. The ability to make choices for a company depends on having access to its data, which can be presented in various formats. When data can be altered for some purpose, whether for marketing or sales, accounting or customer service, these applications make the best use of the data. The ability to alter data in many ways, such as rearranging, sorting, changing, and moving data around, is necessary for accurate data analysis.

10.2: Variations

Many SQL database solutions extend the capabilities of SQL by providing imperative languages, sometimes known as procedural languages. Oracle's PL/SQL & IBM Db2's SQL PL are two examples of these kinds of languages. Data manipulation languages come in various flavors and features depending on the database provider. The American Standards National Institute (ANSI) has developed several guidelines for SQL; however, manufacturers continue to offer adaptations to the standard even though they do not entirely implement it. Two distinct programming languages are used to manipulate data: procedural programming and declarative programming. In the beginning, batch processing languages were exclusively used within computer programs.

However, since the invention of SQL, database administrators have begun to use these languages interactively.

Conclusion

Utilizing and modifying data to develop insights that can assist organizations in solving an issue or discovering possibilities is what is meant by the term "data analysis." Anyone who engages in the data analysis process might be considered a data analyst. Many businesses use the term "data analyst" as a professional job. Cleaning and manipulating data, modeling it in certain formats, and developing visualizations or views to emphasize information that the judgment could use are some of these as an analyst. The most common application of SQL presently is as a foundational architecture that facilitates the creation of user dashboards or reporting tools. Databases can have complicated instructions easily sent to them, and the data within them can be altered in a subject of seconds. Users can present data using intuitive dashboards, which are competent in illustrating data in various ways thanks to the ease with which the software may be used. When performing data analysis using SQL, the querying language of the database interacts simultaneously with numerous databases and uses relational databases. This adaptable language is simple enough for consumers to understand while at the same time offering the level of depth required to make it possible to develop sophisticated dashboards and data analysis tools. SQL can execute complex data analysis despite having a vocabulary that is easy to understand. The 1980s and 1990s got the rise of enterprise resource planning systems, which could handle several thousand daily transactions. Modern cloud-based computing systems are so advanced that they can handle billions of transactions daily. The methods used to collect and process data have significantly increased recently. Whoever understands how to make use of this data has a distinct advantage. Even while the technology that operates in the back has become increasingly complex, the good news is that to make use of it, we do not necessarily need to comprehend the specifics of the system it is built on. There are methods available to you that are straightforward but highly effective, which you can use to accelerate the growth of your company, increase your profits, or earn that promotion you've been eyeing.

Printed by BoD™in Norderstedt, Germany